SKYSI

SKYSPEAK

poems

JAN HELLER LEVI

Louisiana State University Press

Baton Rouge

First Printing

DESIGNER: Amanda McDonald Scallan
TYPEFACE: Galliard
TYPESETTER: G & S Typesetters, Inc.
PRINTER AND BINDER: Edwards Brothers, Inc.

Library of Congress Cataloging-in-Publication Data

Levi, Jan Heller.
 Skyspeak : poems / Jan Heller Levi.
  p. cm.
 ISBN 0-8071-3102-4 (alk. paper) — ISBN 0-8071-3103-2 (pbk. : alk. paper)
 I. Title.
PS3562.E8877S58 2005
811'.54—dc22

2005015567

My thanks to the editors of the following publications, in which these poems, or versions of them, originally appeared: *Big City Lit:* "Theory of Flight: The Adopted Daughter's Version"; *Columbia: A Journal of Literature and Arts:* "About Lips I Am Not So Sure"; *Cortland Review:* "Fall River Historical Museum: Lizzie Speaking"; *drunkenboat.com:* "Untitled (for the moment)," "Wedding Party"; *Lyric:* "The Marvin Gaye Version"; *Mid-American Review:* "This Is Not A Question Specific to The Netherlands"; *New Orleans Review:* "I Lost My Best Friend to Music"; *Noisma:* "Life is A Basket"; *St. Galler Tagblatt:* "Hanging out the Laundry to Dry"; *The Women's Review of Books:* "Anatomy Lesson," "Eve Speaks"; *TriQuarterly:* "Skywatch." My gratitude also to Yaddo, for immense generosity.

"Skywatch" was awarded the George Bogin Memorial Award of the Poetry Society of America in 1998, and "Eve Speaks" was awarded the Writer's Magazine/Emily Dickinson Award in 2001.

With thanks to my friends and my family; and remembering June Jordan.

for Christoph

The mystery begins after all the confessions are made.
—JEAN COCTEAU

CONTENTS

SKYSPEAK

POEM FOR WILLIAM J. MOREHOUSE

Who is this William J. Morehouse
b. 1819
d. 1903
with his four stones set flat in the grass, in the center of this quiet, breathing
*   place?*

Did he have two lives, too?
The first, not as bad as he originally thought?
The second, not quite as he planned?

Here's to his sleep, and to mine, and to others'
all those finished with feeling
all those just beginning to feel again
all those whose hands are still
all those whose hands are still a bit numb

Marie wants to wake up where she can walk outside in her nightgown.
Donna wants Italy.
I want sacred and profane sex, a cigarette after, to know the names of trees,
and to be, perversely,
calmer. But fully alive.
I want the nightgown morning, too.

Donna wants St. Dymphna to cure her.
Marie wants a summer of peace.
I want these things for my friend, and for the friend of my friend.

Donna wants St. Jude to help her find what she's lost.
Marie wants Richard to be able to get his liver transplant.
I want to learn to love the beautiful tree that will not bear fruit.

I want my mother, sometimes, usually late afternoon.
I imagine her coming into a room where I'm hard at work.
I look up and say,
"Hi, Mom, you've been gone a long time."

I want to dance to *Heard It Through the Grapevine* 56 times.
Marie and Donna do too.

My mother kept a notebook,
neatly tabbed into sections

Crazy Glue: second drawer, table to the right of living room couch
Masking Tape: under the sink
Buttons: lilac tin box, mahogany basement hutch

A good wife's prepared for repairing what's broken;
a family's so busy tearing things apart.

For a long time, the things I loved were souvenirs
of the things I feared. A picture of God
above the card table.
The cards themselves,
the sticky King and Queen.
Why should I use your language,
which has been so corrupted?
I ask this in your language.

I came screaming out
of a bathroom—
something about the arrangement of various ointments—
and a father said *shhh, shhh,*
it's going to be all right.
Which it wasn't,
not for a long time.

Yet his chest was so warm,
and my hysterical hair crept onto my neck,
conducive to soothing, and

the lyric, in contrast to the dramatic monologue
(in which there is always a listener
present in the room),
gives us the mind alone with itself.
Lord, that's a big room.

Take away the things I have used,
the dollhouse and all its appointments,

the pipecleaner parents, the matchbox beds,
the transitional objects;
in retrospect, everything
so ridiculous and essential.
A picture of God
installed over the card table.
Then a picture of a picture,
then no picture;
or God.

Like two tall strong buildings which once were there,
and then weren't.

THIS IS NOT A QUESTION
SPECIFIC TO THE NETHERLANDS

1.
We were on the Utrecht line;
a sound like rocks. A minute later,
the train still going, we forgot.
Until we stopped.
Ongeluk.
We don't understand Dutch, but the word for *accident*
doesn't sound very serious. Neither does *depression.*
Neither does *I'd like to be ground up till there's
nothing left of me.*

But this is not a question specific to the Netherlands,
where we just happened to be.
Sticky situation of the month:

some poor soul throws himself on the tracks and you're delayed
while the conductors scrape what's left of him
off the wheels. You're late.

Do you have a right to be annoyed?
And at whom?

2.
An old friend of my father's,
whose wife had died a year before,
at last feels well enough to plan a trip.
Ridiculous to pay for airport parking
for two weeks.
Instead, he asks his sister for a lift.

3.
I'm halfway through *The Diary of Anne Frank* when
our car is the only one to lose its lights.
Now we sit in silence and in black,
making up facts.
Maybe he parked his car by the tracks, or
ran from that island of houses
across the field.

4.
Sister of my father's friend
arrives at brother's apartment at the scheduled hour.
Rings once. Twice.

I still believe people are good at heart,
Anne will say on page 253, if I get there.
Even if I don't.

No response. She tries the key
he gave her sometime back. It works.

Three young conductors
stumble through our darkened coach carrying—
are those pitchforks?

She finds her brother
lying facedown on the kitchen floor in his boxer shorts.
A bread knife in that good heart.

5.
The stars are nasty flecks of light.
The friend who's holding dinner for us checks the clock,
gathers up the plates. She thinks we've stood her up.

No way, my father says, his friend's death was suicide.
He opts, instead, for a story with windows pried or jiggled locks.
James, he says, wasn't the type. What's the type? I ask.

The type who does a thing like that!   Oh. For my father,
that James made his chest a chopping block,
or that my mother, the cancer crawling down her throat,

would up her dose of Darvoset exponentially the night
before the morning she overslept for good, is not
within the realm of possibility. We won't discuss

it. But Dad, that you say James couldn't
(or Mom wouldn't), thus they *didn't*—that's a tautology.
Oh stop it, Jan, stop it. Stop your endless playing with words.

6.

There are, according to no study I could ever find, approx-
imately 141 ways of committing suicide, 47 of them, to varying
degrees, classified as hostile. The gauge is based on complicity,
appearance or affect thereof. Our suicide tonight selected
method #37, rendering us, passengers within the train he threw
himself below, accessories or contributory agencies to his
crime. Something like the pharmacist in my mother's very pop-
ular choice (#2); the belt manufacturer in method #11; the
bridge engineer, the architect of high-rise buildings, the pro-
ducers and distributors of plastic bags (#17, #49, #112, respec-
tively).

7.

Without the aid of Darvoset, Utrecht
starts putting itself to bed. Window lights
are blinking out, family cats are slinking
under backdoor screens to stalk their mice.
A few children are whining for one more
story. No, not a different one, the same one,
over. Children like the same creepy
ogre arriving night after night, the same dumb
cluck pointing to a sky that's falling, falling.
My mother, turning the pages when I was young,
read *with expression,* as we used to say.
Cancer of the tongue took that away.
If I squint into the window of this stalled train,
I can almost see a bit of her
in my reflection. But with my eyes open,
I know that's absurd. I'd never have
the guts to do what she did, or my father's
friend, James. Though I spent half my life bent
on achieving the despair that such courage
requires. *Oh stop it, Jan, stop it.*
Stop playing with words.

8.
The conductors on the Utrecht line
are teenage boys in uniform. They dispense
and collect tickets, announce stops
and, from time to time,
scrape the sticky flesh
and jangled bones of a suicide
off the axles.

The trip from Amsterdam to Utrecht
takes one-half hour. Or three.
Depending.

Some nights the engineer,
a gentle man, he'd never hurt a flea,
he's not the type,
goes home a murderer.

THEORY OF FLIGHT
THE ADOPTED DAUGHTER'S VERSION

Plane, I was born on you, and I remember.
Flying bus, stork, I swam in your arms,
swayed, rocked.
I was cooed and swaddled.
I gazed up into my parent's faces,
the clouds,
and blinked with pleasure.
And it was you, plane,
who swept me up and carried me again
twenty-four years, one hour 24 miraculously short, too-long
minutes later from gate
to gate to Suite 1101 West, M.D.
Anderson Cancer Hotel,
my mother's black breath
puffing into the Houston air.
as she sits, politely
dying in the chair over by the window.

Now I have luggage that has become ordinary.
Now I read magazines 17,000 feet above the earth.
Now I pee into disappearing turquoise water.
Now handsome men reassure me about turbulence.

Plane, I was born on you,
and I remember.
Though they say this is impossible,
I remember your fleecy seatbacks,
feasts of celebration rolling down a narrow aisle.
Out of a shining womb in the sky,
I came into my life.
Thus it is ordained I should sing
your praises, hosanna of your sturdy span
and various devices
all the days of my life.
And for the theory of flight that put seven non-stops, daily,
into the metastasizing heavens
and back down into Texas, I bless
my strange birth
and bless most its vehicle.

Thursday afternoon, Houston, the excavators
drop their picks and shovels down her throat.
Thursday evening, my parents call New York.
No need for you to come,
my mother says in her scorched voice,
let's see what the doctors say
tomorrow. I sleep and dream.
The doctors came to me with their long necklaces
dangling. I wake, call,
say, I'm not waiting.
There's a midnight flight that gets in at eleven.
Oh, she says, and then, oh again,
and then my mother, who was never greedy,
who never in her life asked for any more than she was given,
including a child born out of her own womb, then my mother asks,
Oh, do you think there's any way you can get here sooner?

THAT WAS THE FALL

when mattress salesmen became sleep consultants,
when we put all the ballots in a locked box
and steamed it closed,
when the Captain and Maria climbed over that mountaintop
and tumbled down into the workcamp,
when the tree outside the window grew rampant, lush,
hostile, and magnificent,
when one of my students said,
"from the very first class, I knew you were alive,"
and I thought, *oh baby, I'm so alive it's killing me.*

LIPS

Notepad for kisses
Ledge of the unspoken
Companion to the village idiot teeth

It is from this you adopted your laughable equation for integrity

Because you are the part
of the body both inside and out
because you are divided from yourself when pleasure comes

how it would come to rely on you
how it would leave you
not like that at all

Which is you?

See page 41 for a discussion of the story
in which there is a fire.
One reader thinks it no fire at all,
just some twigs and wood arranged coincidentally, albeit
incipiently.
Then on page 55, someone asks a question
that could start a fire burning
or put it out.

Lips, you have always been an arsonist at heart.

(or maybe just wood stacked in the fireplace)

and when someone said I sing of you, use your village idiot teeth
incomparable   incompatible
Twins of tomorrow
flooded hyacinths
gates   gatekeepers

   but when,
unpersuaded to do so

something blossoms   it seems right
 it should be so

and when someone asked,
and the answer to the question was. . .

   I never

tasted such conjoining of wetness until the moment that followed
the previous less conjoined, less wet moment
Don't pretend you don't

know what I mean

But maybe we did,
amidst wars and famine

imagine our wars, our famine   ·
more pronounced
In the local is the universal

I once believed about art
if the pencil was tossed upon the bed

you wrote about the bed

That's what I always think about diffident people.
It never occurs to me, and won't, even if you insist,
that the man who looks at me with sleepy eyes
isn't sleepy. This is not about romance.

This is about history. This is about pushing my eyes so far in
with the back of my hands
that I see China, those adorable straw hats.
Farthest place away, and I didn't want to go there

nor stay here

Hypercatalectic. Velvety, but not overly

so undersides of needlepoint pillows tossed to the side
which is the center of the family romance, which
is not about romance,

it's about history. Pseudo-identical ballads supreme, rhymed
demitasses, no sugar, but a little

salt. Into these 24-hour stores,

dreams pour.
As children, we heard too much: the scream of pennies,

hair crying on the brush,
the crispy goodbye of a cigarette. Overnight, the fuzzy caterpillars
were gone. Her breath was tobacco-y and sweet.

I'd captured them that evening in a Hellman's Mayonnaise jar,
stabbed the blue metal top with breathing holes.

TONGUE

(effectively, that is)

for any distraction

beyond the four doors of our sight:
love, fear, abandonment, change.

Suicide, the she-poet said,
is a lazy desire for rebirth.
Hallowed be thy name.
The asters stick their ruddy, blurred faces into the sky.
Our knees are black with them, so we kneel

to be one with something, if only the dark.

SKYWATCH

Between Aries and Andromeda lies the small constellation Triangulum, the triangle. The most important object here is the 33rd object in Messier's catalogue, described as a hazy white glow of almost uniform brightness.

—*New York Times,* Week of November 3

Who is this Messier and how do I get
his catalogue? This week my
stars swerved like New
York cabbies. You tell
them where to go
and they take you.
Sometimes. Where
can I find Monsieur
Messier, with his
dossier of objets d'sky?
I've had too much
coffee this week, too
much frothy cappuccino
which is a vile
drink, not to mention
institution.
I thought I saw my major
ex- across a room
at a poetry reading
but it was only
a hazy white glow of almost uniform
brightness.
Who is this Messier?
Physicists must know him,
or meteorologists.
I'm probably only 3 degrees
of separation from someone
who slept with him,
or his wife,
now there would be a messy love
triangulum.
Here are, I think,
the first 14 of the 33 objects
in Messier's catalogue:

1. the rubber-stamped constellation that sings:
   "You are not an idiot"
2. young hair
3. the H's behind our knees
4. the astronaut pen that writes upside down
5. house with its face split open, cut lip of bedroom,
   bleeding parlor
6–14. the Scottsboro Boys, all nine of them—pinwheeled
   in the heavens, arms and legs reeling. Especially
   Clarence Norris, 18, who *Life* Magazine, 1937,
   called *the dandy of the outfit, . . . plasters his hair*
   with strong-perfumed grease, keeps his shirt and
   overalls neat and clean.

Unlucky stars, are those lights in the trees,
or rain?
Are those stars in the heavens,
or the buttons of overalls,
polished neat and clean?
Professor Messier, I assume,
would know.
Last summer
the palm reader
took my hand
in his,
traced out a comet's tail.
My skin flamed
with an almost uniform
heat.
This is your life line,
he said. It breaks
off here, but then
begins again. Here.
He looked at me
with some concern.
Expect some great change
in the middle
of your life, he said.
I'm older than you think,
I said,
it's already happened;

I already died.
He consulted no book,
no manual,
but when he touched his fingers
to my brow,
I swear I saw 7 objects
of Messier's catalogue
swirling celestially
behind my eyes:

15. Madame Messier's suitcase. Packed. She's leaving.
    He spends too much time with his head in the clouds.
16. A copy of *Leaves of Grass* from the Texas Book Depository.
17. The little engine that tried, but couldn't.
18. My dead sainted mother's underwear, a hazy white glow of
    almost uniform brightness.
19. The idealist who writes his love in the dust.
20. The pick-ax still quivering in Trotsky's brain.
21. A window in Robert McNamara's Pentagon office, 1965.
    He turns to see my distant Quaker cousin, Norman
    Morrison, douse himself with gasoline on the plaza
    below, and set himself afire.

What is the difference between desire and ambition?
Desire, I think, is a river,
ambition a boat,
but in a hazy glow, the river mist takes
the form of a boat,
and sails you
away from
ambition.
In fact, it was my major
ex- I saw,
from the window of a cab.
Uptown, downtown,
from the perspective
of the Great Galaxy
in Andromeda, known
as sector M31,
whose separation
from earth is a mere

750,000 light-years.
I hopped out at the nearest
park bench,
sector M33,
from which Earth would be
a faint curiosity.
Indeed it was.
And odd it was
that she was
carrying a papoose.
And I-Ruined-Your-Life
came and sat down
beside me. And
I-Plucked-You-From-
Safety-and-Threw-
You-to-the-Wolves
said, Hey, how have you
been. And I answered
cordially. Cordially
mind you.
Then she drew
from her papoose
a woolen blanket,
more than all the colors
of Joseph's coat.
We lay down in the great
sheep meadow,
our ankles, hips,
and shoulders touching.
The sky came close,
like a doctor with a thermometer.
Messier's milky waters
and boats swam into our eyes.
Look, she said, there it is:

22. Your heterosexuality, a little tattered, but still usable.

And I said, what?

And she said,
look, there it is:

23. Your own divided heart, its chambers of desire and chambers of dread
    overlapping.

And I said, what?

And she said,
look, there it is:

24. The amethyst bauble at the throat of Countess Gemini in *Portrait of a
    Lady*. "She lived," Henry James wrote, "it might be said, at the window of
    her spirit, but now she was leaning far out."

Oh, I said,
I thought it might
be something like that,
and she said,
look, I've got to be going.
I said, what,
again?
And she said
yeah, and left.

Lucky stars,
you've been dead so long and still
you shine,
apples in the night
from the tree of regret.
Madame Messier has packed her bags,
and is moving on.
When I left my husband,
a friend said
don't do it,
before you know it
you'll be one of those
dames in their 40s,
alone and bitter,
taking taxicabs,
knowing exactly what to tip.
Last night,
reading about Messier's catalogue,
I thought about the story

of our lives,
the ones we tell ourselves
about ourselves,
how they're packed with themes,
but so few symbols.
I thought I'd make a list
of things, of objects,
the ones we carry with us,
the ones we leave behind.
But the columns wouldn't
split properly,
I wanted two boxes,
I kept getting a triangle.

Once I was in Eden and I walked, blithely,
out of it.
How was I to know?
There seemed another Eden,
just next door. It looked familiar,
and I was tired of the new.
All day he strolled around with his name-tags.
Glitter turned specific, but I craved
the blobbiness of things,
the inexact borders,
the possibility that this could also be

that. Of course I was an idiot. I'd run back
now if I could bear his painless
children, even call the girl *If Only,*
the boy, *I Told You So.*
Instead of living in this okay crowded world,
I'd make all my mistakes in Paradise.
Is that possible?
Is it?
I didn't even see the gate.
Then the gate closed.

LIFE IS A BASKET

Life is a basket, you said.
It was not a directive,
it was philosophy, an image
that worked. We were at an exhibit
of writing implements through the ages.
Amazing, the variety of pencils.
I had to bite my lip to keep
from touching you.

So I asked something. Flat out.
But in phrasing so elliptical,
we were both covered. That's when
you answered life
is a basket etc., with a shrug
of your shoulders so scrutable—

—thirty seconds later—what
took us so long?—we were slamming
out of that museum and into
the closest bar, your hands
on my breasts, my thighs, my face, my lips;
mine nested deep and tight in the heat
between your hips.
When you put me in that taxi an hour later . . .

. . . I can't think of anything wronger
than the whole affair.
Including the two dozen long-stemmed red roses, utterly
romantic and savage of you, months
later you could walk down a whole street without
holding my hand, to say, "I'm not
the touching kind," so I could say,

"Oh."
But what about those Sundays,
me sitting on the side of your bed,
pulling on my infidel socks?
Rhetorical question.
Life is a basket and we were just—shrug—
filling it up.

WHAT BECOMES OF THE BROKEN-HEARTED

What becomes of the broken-hearted
is that we do it ourselves.
Hammers under pillows.
We pull out the hammer
for our morning clunkety-clunk. You were walking with me,
steady as a candle,
autumny as sky,
toward a swimming pool.
I don't know how a swimming pool got into my dream.

What never gets into the story are the things you're ashamed of,
but they peep out of the story.
Like the doctor's desire for a juicy disease pops out of a boring diagnosis.

What becomes of the broken-hearted
is that we build the world.
Out of our sorrow,
out of our lack of: outlines, file cards, good study habits.
Children, don't you know what you're getting into,
going to school everyday with your lunchbox
bumping rhythmically on your thigh?
Here's the bruise, it's the shape
of a hand-held tape recorder.
Turn it on, and it's your father's voice,
scratchy like the nineteenth century,
saying *shh, shhh,*
it's going to be okay,

you're going to like this,
you're going to learn to love this.

See, I told you I can't tell a story straight
and this story is not about abuse,
not the kind you're thinking, anyway—

but you said we have an abusive relationship,
that was the day your shrink crawled into bed with us,
oh it was crowded in there,
what with your mother, my mother, maybe half a father between us—

Then I dive, or you dive, or we dive,
and the clear water separates.

The man with the leg cut off just below the knee
twists out of the pool, dripping.
All his leg hair, matted down on that slick, pointy stump,
points down horribly into the blue syllables.

What becomes of the broken-hearted is repetition,
regress, coupled with the inability to tell a story straight through,
My qualifiers climb skyward off

like drops of water from a big, friendly dog shaking the pool water out
of his coat.

Or a castrated man, I mean amputated, not castrated,
when he pulls himself out of the pool, he might shake too,
and drops of water jettison off,
land somewhere else

the color of a door slamming

THE DAILY NEWS

Two evenings and twenty-six years ago,
Kath and I curled on a couch.
Complaining, as usual.
I say something about a certain circle of writers and
she says, Oh I feel so far from all that. We agree: nothing
ever happens in those poems
except
little epiphanies in gardens.

The next morning it's the early '80s,
Laurie's East Village apartment.
Ken and I love her fruit and vegetable wallpaper:
eggplants, apples, and jaunty sprigs of parsley
dancing over their names in four different languages.
We're sharing Laurie's pork-chop breakfast
when my bag falls off the table, spilling
Amelia Earhart's journal at our feet.
Women of my generation are crazy about her:
she went everywhere, ended up nowhere.

That evening it's the cusp of the decade.
I just so happen to fall in love with a woman,
the woman dumps me, there's a jumble
of events in here that I don't feel
like going into at this time; let's
just say I was not at my best.
All I wanted to do was sleep,
which is what I did, more or less,
for seven years. When I wake up,

it's 1995, my arm itches from shoulder
to wrist, I scratch it
by writing some poems.
They tell pieces of this story in
inaccurate order, a rhetorical strategy
that the speaker of this poem
is still attempting to refine
or abandon.

Today, just as I finish,
without cheating,
Puzzle #4 ("Strained Relations")
in my circa 1978 Daily News Jumbo Book of Crossword Puzzles,
learning that deipnosophists
are table-talkers and nehus are Hawaiian anchovies,
Linda calls.

We talk about our grandmothers. I had
two good ones, one a little better.
She had a good one and a bad one, the bad one
smelled like dress shields.
Then we talk about Scott's last expedition.
The ice, the hopelessness, the honor.
We make a plan to get together and deipnosophize next week.
Before we hang up,
Linda asks if I could discover anything, anything
in the world that hasn't already been discovered,
what would it be?
and this poem answers

a new emotion

You know how it is: August, the pears
all at once too heavy for their
branches; everything bending down,
down. And what doesn't fall on its own
is simply calling for a little help:
a finger tap, or the patient, constant heave
of an ax. So the thing that gets you, come on,
admit it, is not that I did it.
Or didn't. No.
It's what you can't stop
seeing in these photographs:
the expectant tilt of his head
toward the door, her almost ecstatic
embrace of the floor.

You know how it is: one Sunday morning,
just like any other, some father,
just like any other, might be taking a snooze
on the horsehair sofa while his wife, above,
offers up the last minutes of her
hospital-cornering to eleven plunges
of a toolshed blade. Well, what family
doesn't have its little problems?
When the parlor door creaks open
to trouble his sleep,
his feather brows twitch and rise,
but not precisely in surprise.
A perfect gentleman to the last,
"Finished with mother, have you?" he asks.

IT STARTED IN RAGE

which is concrete. The scream
of a bathroom door; only one time
did you hold me in your arms
(like I dreamed all day,
all night, without knowing it,
you might) like that:
my woman head against
your man chest, the two stern
mesas of your breasts
hot as the earth, and me,
long weary traveler,
laid there my weary
head to rest.
Impedimence of stone,
only now I understand:
to keep the horrors from me,
you kept them in your heart.

But that it started in love,
and goes on in dreams that twist
love obediently each night,
is intellectual,
i.e., obvious,
like recantations
of buttons we don't push,
phone calls we don't take,
letters we don't open
but don't send back—
oh it goes on and on
because we are so ambitious
and diligent.

Two weeks ago,
when you spoke to me
with an enthusiasm
I hadn't heard for years,
my heart opened, just a crack.
Two frail ova
strung on a telephone wire,

or two leopards circling one another,
which of the two images
are we? Because we are both,
we will always be
both.

After I hung up,
whatever it was
was gone again.
Kindler and kindling
of the most polite fury,
I stoke your flame.
We live far from one another,
I live where it often rains.
I walked down to the stream,
watched a ripple licking
and licking one rock.
I watched a long time,
trying to turn it back to water and stone,
but it stayed fire.

UNTITLED (for the moment)

If we hate our parents, who made us, isn't that
a way of hating ourselves? My father, for ex-
ample. I made a career of cataloging
his injustices, and yes, they were legion. Here's
a recap: the tongue depressors, the rigid heart,
oreo cookies slashed in two, their plastic wrap-
pers trembling. The tampax string. The litter inci-
dent. The mission. The misdiagnosis. Mostly,
the misapprehension of my twisting, like a plant,
toward the sun. He saw only the twisting. How he
scorned my larval, alchemical spirit. Oh yes,
the days are wonderfully similar, dull and

horrible in that suburban steambox called my
childhood, he the pillar, the post, the key-jangler,
the money-bags, the bookie, the Politburo,
the President, the Archduke Ferdinand, the King,
the King of Kings, I the wee thing, the holy roller,
the short-division problem, the toothless
and the over-toothed, the carwash
drinker, the vomiting medusa, the screamer,
the drop in the bucket, the poet. This
has all been chronicled. Now my pop is ancient,
a lambie-kins, a *pfuft-pfut* flat tire. Across banquet
rooms at family affairs, I watch him nod and
bob at cousins, nieces and nephews, taking in

maybe half, giving out less. We all agree that
he's adorable, demented elder statesman
of our tribe. We finish his lost-in-space
sentences for him; pretend not to notice
his tea-dribbled tie. But what I want to say
is oh scourge of my youth, where have you gone?
Now that I am strong enough to win, you've
disappeared into this doddering, sweet, infuriating
shade that I'd be a bully to pick on. All bent over
like that, you sneaky bastard. Come on, stand up,
I know you're inside. Come out and fight like a man.
We were something back then, remember, all thunder,

lightning and fireworks. Come on out, you fist
in a glove, be who you've always been: my tall, my strong,
my awful, my greatest enemy, my love.

VARANASI
Renée

How incredibly filthy it is, she says, you cannot imagine.
Our guide put us into the boat, then left. Terry said, Can you believe it?—

To come all this way just to be abandoned by another man!
My sister visits the river of life and death. She floats on typhoid.

It was evening. A funeral. Whole families come down to the blissful,
    muddy shores,
she said. They burn their dead. This I knew,

but to hear it from her, my sister, was different.
I saw a dozen flaming campfires, I heard the singing,

I slipped the sister ring, golden as the Ganges, on her finger,
and we were wed.

She was searching for her father in the land of her birth.
This was a detour.

We wore the saris, the ones with the tunics and legs,
she said. The fires sparkled up and down the river.

All night the ashes flow into the river.
The next morning the whole family will be back,

bathing in the river, brushing their teeth.
We saw that too, she said.

LAZARUS

I.

Purple was your favorite word and mine, complicit.

Not for you, but for me.
It's simple: I miss you.

I go down to your grave, your locker.
Dried flowers about it: I misread
their colors; what time has done to pink
I call blush.

I see you: eyes,
crook of elbow on the statue in that photograph,
back I'd know anywhere
like I'd know a tree, or a song
by the first notes before the words begin.
Your legs, your ribcage.
Your handsome penis.
But most of all, your fragrant mouth.

Come up, I call. I can't believe the silence,
the birds croak into it.

Come up. And you do.
Without ceremony,
as when the conductor emerges from the car
ahead of yours.

Since you died in summer, I've brought a heavy coat,
boots for your numb feet,

but they are warm, they are warm.

2.
They are warm, they are warm,
these winter evenings, our hands, your fingers
I really can't remember, but these will do

carrying the cup to your lips. You are the village
attraction, the people come to stare
but not to touch, the beaded curtain

of our tent clicks like teeth. I make
love to you in the purple night; it is unsatisfying
on one level, all I desired

on another. You don't have to press your palms
to my back, make speeches, get a job —
just being dead here is all that's required of you.

3.
I am famous. I have stretched my hand into the light
and brought back darkness.

4.
But after a while, you become like any man.
You have needs.

Reed was one of the first to go.
Before it had a name, his bones started turning to paper.
It's not true it didn't have a name.
The doctors gave it a dozen.
First shin splints, next shingles, then rheumatoid arthritis.
Maybe a tumor, or collection of tumors. Followed
by combinations of the above, to which were added
some kind of blood thing, or virus.
They kept testing. We kept waiting.
They kept naming. We repeated the names
like children in a spelling bee,
sounding out the letters in our mouths like a mantra.

Then he was up again, same old Reed,
heading to the clubs,
bringing us languid, humid stories from the baths,
showing up at our wedding party,
coolest guest of all,
gentlest guy in the world head-to-toe in leather
with a pack of pick-ups trailing behind,
gentlest kids in the world
head-to-toe in leather. Good dancers, too.
I remember they stayed after everyone else was gone,
helped us clean up,
scraping lasagna from paper plates,
downing the last of the wine in pale blue plastic glasses.

When they left,
they tossed our garbage bags over their shoulders
and clomped down the stairs,
Santa Clauses in reverse.
Two weeks later the phone tree
told us the flu,
two weeks later, worse.
Two weeks later
back in the hospital,
howling from the weight of the sheets on his skin.

At the funeral home, he wasn't in leather,
but his favorite plaid workshirt and jeans. Casual, comfortable.

If the boys from our party were there,
I didn't recognize them.
Or maybe they'd already left.
Ken and I arrived late, after the service, stayed a few minutes,
went out for coffee, went home.
Since then, the friends who connected us to Reed
have drifted out of our lives—
there's no name for how that happens.
Now the marriage is over, too.
Still, when I think of Reed,
I can taste the last crumb of wedding cake on my lips
when we kissed goodbye that night,
how sweet it was,
how goddamn, goddamn sweet.

ANATOMY LESSON

If you could have things just the way you wanted,
every part of you would be detachable.
Your heart, which doctors call a muscle
& they must be right, plops out of your chest,
rolls its way across the floor with a funny plud plud
plud to the typewriter, heaves itself up on the keys.
It flops & writhes & the words come up
like punches on the page. Meanwhile,
you have to pee. Your bladder
grows tiny legs, scampers to the bathroom,
hovers over the toilet seat. Your hands
sprout little wings, go flying after it, clutch it, lift
& squeeze. Out comes the piss, like water
from a soapy sponge. Oh, that's
delightful. Meantime, remember, your heart
is still writing. Now you'd like a suntan. Your
bare arms & legs take the elevator down
to the park, lay themselves out across
a bench, rotate every fifteen minutes
between the prime tanning hours of 11 & 2.
Your right breast takes the subway
downtown to your husband's studio, your left
breast hops the shuttle to Boston to be
cupped in the hand of a former lover. Your
clit is checking into a hotel room in Cannes
with the tongue of the very young Paul Newman.
Meantime, remember, your heart is still writing.
Your hands are now free to join a phone tree
& stuff envelopes for Greenpeace. Your feet
are dancing to the Marvin Gaye version of
Heard It Through the Grapevine, your chest is
slipping on a tee-shirt that says *No Justice,
No Peace* & heading for the street. Meantime,
your heart, your fabulous, brilliant, complicated,
undistracted heart is writing, writing, writing.

HANGING OUT THE LAUNDRY TO DRY

The sun is high in the sky,
vivid, livid, but kind. When the Master makes His appearance, He doesn't always

shine. I say the sad music, the music like water, the music that makes Buddha
anxious, the flip of the tuxedo tails when the Master

polishes His behind.
I want to be happy, will be too, wearing somebody's socks,
nobody's shoes.

ANYWHERE OR SWITZERLAND

Great golf courses of nature and Swiss industriousness,
my husband, in his Mitsubishi van, winds through you today.

He's got one foot on the gas pedal, the other on the brake,
one hand steering. The other hand is free, for the reflexes

he doesn't have. At a curve or an incline, he slips a palm
under his thigh, to lift, then align. I have watched him do this.

So naturally. Like we walk. Easily, not
thinking. Not struck dumb by our casual stride across a room

to pick up a cup of coffee, answer the phone, open a window.
Neither amazed nor proud of our achievement,

the against-all-odds commerce between desire and deed.
Not humbled by the countless messages transmitted, relayed, received,

translated; , commands of brain, kisses of neuron to neuron,
synchronicities, requests, conversions, conversations, dis-

engagements and resumptions of intimacies, *Sie*s become
*du*s—and we Do! Walk.

But not him. Not my husband. Not easily,
nor as much nor as well as he used to. There is no cure,

the doctors say, for the dimming connections on his line.
Sometimes I think of course there isn't. The diagnosis is life;

whatever has been given can, will, be taken away.
To my husband, driving through Switzerland or anywhere,

I offer praise and honor for the lesson his life teaches:
let us use, at every given moment, what we have left.

THE EARTH-STOPPER

1.
Home for what we want to catch
is a sly black hole.
The night before the hunt,
I plug up the holes,
so my lady's foxes have nowhere to go.

2.
It is raining. What tantrum
            of pleasure, what flute in the wilderness
            (all of a one-thingness, yet multiple) that threatens,

    that soothes. How the leaves
            reckon with the restlessness above, how
            they shiver, how they sigh. Resistance

    and release
            makes the music God most loves. Now forget
            those stymied fluencies in conjugation with the summer

    breeze. Turn your (reckless)
face to reinstate what I remember most
            about this scene. The moon. Moon

    is the scene! Feeding the earth, bosomy
dream, all the radiance that thrives

    in her hair
            and/or skin and/or blue eye
            of her sky—oh my oh my oh my oh my oh my—

    Pity we can't touch
            what touches us. Pity
            we are human. Pity you can't walk into this picture

    with me.
            But decent that you try.

3.
Partners: tears and illumination.
Mystery and persuasion.
Foxes. Foxholes.

My father was an earth-stopper, and his father before him.
Honest work, to tip the odds.
And the tools so rudimentary—

the slender spade,—

4.

    the throbbing lantern!

5.
In another century, you'll lay down
like green grass,
talk your lips irresponsible.
This has its beauty, too.

6.
My first wife I left, my second left me.
The world goes round laconically.
Sometimes I think the foxes are like dreams.
The shrill screams
that are music to my lady's dead
ears rivet mine to my sweat-stained bed—

7.
I am the earth-stopper, quiet and calm.
This is my song. Trust is never far
beyond betrayal. The door you thought
was home does not slam shut, just disappears.
Did you ever have a home at all?

I am the earth-stopper, the one
who keeps the quarry here.
My work takes place at night,
while all the world sleeps.
When else would we stop the world
and pitch it forward again?

Our loyalties, divided, should at least be instructive.
All waking is hunting.
All sleeping is being pursued
by the you not yet you.

8.
       —Moon, moon, you cast your breath on me!

All any of us ask to do our dark work
(not only the digging but filling)

the light to see by

I LOST MY BEST FRIEND TO MUSIC

I lost my best friend to music.
In the 41st year of her life, she
disappeared into strings, chords,
minor and major, the cello's
redolent moan.
There was a man involved (as there often is).
Though he bought the tickets, and his hair
is the color of a burnished clarinet,
I don't hold him responsible.

I lost my best friend to music.
It was a fairly-distributed loss;
some chamber, some symphonic.
In the 42nd year of our lives,
we are bound to lose something,
and my loss could have been worse:
I might have lost a child, if I'd had one,
or a limb,
or a breast. Still,

I railed against losing.
Tried to follow her at first,
into CD clubs and subscription concerts,
and crushes on violinists;
brushed up on my composers,
which ones died penniless, which ones mad,
which ones both, with horrible syphilis too.

I couldn't keep up.
There was always more music, more versions, more interpretations.
Just as I had mastered Radu Lupu, there was Brendel and Pollini.
Maria Callas ripped my heart out and threw it around the room.

Then one day
I heard Jussi Bjoerling and Robert Merrill,
in the famous duet from Bizet's *Pearl Fishers,* and
I was done for.
Each note unfolding into the next,
the journey, the patience of the flute,

like the breath of the body,
held deep in the body,
escaping,
up,
while those two men
share the longest,
saddest,
extended sigh
in the history
of the human voice.

And what are they singing about?
The liner notes say a woman who threatens their friendship, which they vow
    to uphold.
But I say they're singing life,
how we're always losing something,
how beautiful that is.